WIRED TO LEAD

WIRED TO LEAD:

It's not just in some of us, but in all of us.

Zayn Mitchell Knaub

NOTE FROM THE AUTHOR

"He asked, "What makes a man a writer?" "Well," I said, "it's simple. You either get it down on paper, or jump off a bridge."

— Charles Bukowski

The process of writing this book has been one of the most fulfilling experiences of my life. I reflected on almost every positive and negative experience or relationship I have had. I reflected on my values, my profession, my choices, my thoughts, my desires, my life, and my death. It has CONSUMED ME for the last year as I felt a roar building up inside of me and an idea aching to breathe the cool night air. Who knows whether this will resonate with anyone else? I hope so. But I recognize now that this idea of flipping over the table of conventional leadership wisdom has been and will continue to be my life's work. I wrote this book for everyone I've ever witnessed be dismissed or quieted by a "superior." I wrote this book as a counterweight to the billion dollar industry trying to select for and teach only "an elite few" the principles and tactics of leadership. I wrote this book for the young men and women looking at the world and asking questions- frustrated and desperately searching for hope in a world that can seem devoid of light more and more every day. Look inside yourself. You hold the answer. The way you respect yourself and your voice. The way you find awareness, inspiration, and accountability for that gift only you can uniquely provide the world.

You are the one you've been waiting for. Start the Revolution.

- Zayn (from an unfinished basement in Nebraska, 18 Dec 2019)

ACKNOWLEDGEMENTS

I'm standing on the shoulders of giants here. All the good that this book gives should be credited to those closest to me that were willing to pour their time, energy, and feedback into it. If this book comes up short, it is due to my own shortcomings.

My wife, my children, my mom and dad, my brothers and close friends. Thank you for your continued friendship and inspiration.

AN INTRODUCTION

It was 2011 and I was new to the organization. I had just been selected for a Special Operations Intelligence Squadron whose missions included supporting counterterrorism (CT) and counterinsurgency (COIN) operations. The responsibilities included direct support to hostage rescues, capture/kill missions, and evacuations of personnel from any U.S. embassies under attack. At the time, I was one year removed from the United States Air Force Academy, whose mission is to "develop leaders of character." I had spent the last year training to become an intelligence officer in central Texas, and my newlywed wife, our two dogs, and I had just arrived at my first non-training, "operational" assignment.

The first missions I was part of was like nothing I had ever seen nor expected. Even though we were thousands of miles from where the missions actually took place, I could follow-along via extensive overhead sensors and close radio and text-based communications with the special operators. The movement, communications, and execution of the mission seemed unbelievably well-choreographed. But at the same time I was fully aware of the amount of uncertainty involved and the speed necessary to carry out these missions. How the hell were the teams thinking so fast? Given the environmental conditions (pitch-black, unfamiliar territory and terrain, uncertain enemy and weapons, highly-dynamic, etc), it was baffling how graceful the operators were and how operationally effective the missions were overall.

For quite a few years, I thought it came down to level of training, technology, or team member talent. But those are all contributing factors rather than the root cause of the effectiveness. Looking back at over a decade of experience in Special Operations, the Intelligence Community, and Silicon Valley, I go back to one principle I've seen consistently transform a group of individuals into elite teams operating at the highest levels of performance: the principle that everyone is a leader.

A few months after being in that first operational organization, I was asked to be the Intelligence Lead for an upcoming mission. This involved coordinating closely with the operational commanders and entire teams of special operators as we planned and rehearsed the operation's execution. During a lull in the planning, I asked one of the team members why he thought they could consistently operate at such a high level, mission after mission. He thought for a few moments and then responded, "You know, it really comes down to the fact that we can't possibly know exactly what is coming next. We do our best to train and prepare, but once the door gets kicked in then it's the person who knows what to do next that is leading us."

I thought about that answer for years, and was reminded of it every single time that I was managing teams in complex environments. Even though I was positionally "The Leader," top-down control was never feasible, let alone a successful strategy. Our team had to move too fast to stay relevant. Our team would face too much uncertainty to engineer success through planning every detail. Instead, I tried to embrace the first principles of what that Operator had explained to me. When facing any ambiguous or complex problem, the best teams are the ones that instill leadership into every single team member. I began reading everything I could about leadership, management, and organizations, searching for this concept that everyone is a leader. I could not find any material that specifically explores this topic and the implications. I actually found the opposite. The overwhelming percentage of leadership and management publications focus on leadership development of an elite few.

All of my experiences told me that everyone is a leader, but it is rarely discussed or nurtured within organizations. Doesn't it seem that the vast majority of managers, officers, and politicians lead through fear instead of trust? Fear of missing a promotion, or getting re-elected, or looking like they made a mistake? In the last four years, I began reading and researching the fundamentals of leadership, influence, and consciousness in order to compare the published evidence against my own experiences. It turns out that the industrial model of leadership, characterized by leader-follower, top-down, and hierarchical paradigms, is a house of cards and does not stand up to scrutiny.

Every single one of us is designed to reflect, imagine, and move toward our greatest hopes and desires. Each one of us can take ownership of our systems of influence and lead ourselves and others. All day. Every day. We are wired to lead.

Over the past three decades, neuroscientists and psychologists have gained more insights into one of the most complex systems in the world: the human mind. In general, there are three neural networks that constitute leadership: awareness, inspiration, and accountability. And these three neural networks operate at two levels within our minds: conscious and unconscious. Leveraging those facts, an individual is able to not only view their world from the lens of a leader, but also begin to optimize the system of influence that exists within the neural networks and at both the conscious and unconscious levels.

We are wired to lead, but only some people do. Some of us refuse to take responsibility for our lives, our thoughts, our goals, and how we are going to get there. If you and the people around you engage the world as leaders, then you are no longer a bystander. When you engage the world as a leader, you are no longer apathetic toward your neighbor, your community, your co-workers, your family. When you engage the world as a leader, then there is unlimited potential to affect the change you seek. **We desperately need a leadership revolution that democratizes leadership to the individual.** Younger generations look at traditional family, political, religious, education, and economic institutions with cynicism. But these institutions provided our parents and their parents a sense of structure within which to grow and seek change. Psychologists and neuroscientists have provided evidence for an individual's inherent ability to affect change, aspire, create and influence. We are wired to lead. **If there is a call to action associated with this book, it is for each and every one of us to consistently take responsibility for the way we influence ourselves and others.**

Whether you are an entry-level employee at a massive corporation, or a stay-at-home parent, or a teenager living with your parents, or a student, or a customer service agent, or a brother or sister, or husband or wife, you are a leader. You have tremendous capacity to influence the outcomes you seek. This book is intended to re-frame your view of leadership, inspire you to take responsibility for your own influence, and introduce you to the system that already exists in your mind so you can fully access your capacity to lead.

PART I

A
LEADERSHIP
REVOLUTION

Chapter 1: INFLUENCE

"The first and greatest victory is to conquer oneself"

- Plato

Picture yourself sitting in a small classroom in Brooklyn Heights, New York. Its Day 1 of the First Grade, early August, and the air conditioner is struggling to keep up. You look around to see the other twenty-five boys and girls who are just as nervous and excited as you. Mr. Barrett, your teacher, walks toward you and tosses a ball of blue yarn.

"Hold on to that end and toss the ball to anyone else in the class," says Mr. Barrett.

You hold on tightly to your piece and toss the ball to a girl just in front of you and to your left. Mr. Barrett repeats the instructions to the girl and she holds on to her piece and passes it to a boy to her left. On and on this goes until there is a web of blue that connects every single student in the classroom. The last student holds on to his portion of the blue yarn and throws the ball back to the teacher. Mr. Barrett then asks you to pull on the end that you still nervously clutch. You do it and see a few of the people, including the girl just in front of you and to the left, move slightly as they keep hold of their piece but are pulled toward you.

Mr. Barrett then asks, "If any of us pull on the yarn, everyone else feels it move, right?"

You and your classmates all nod in agreement.

Mr. Barrett finishes the exercise by explaining "All of your choices, all of your actions, large or small, will affect not only yourself but also everyone else." (this story was inspired by a passage in Priya Parker's The Art of the Gathering)

This story is my preferred allegory for leadership. It is the simplest and most profound demonstration of what I mean by "everyone is a leader." Incredibly, there are hundreds of definitions of leadership. Definitions that include words like motivation, position, charisma, heroes, rank, and "turning vision into reality." But, if we follow Occam's Razor (which espouses the simplest explanation is likely the most accurate one) then John Maxwell's definition of leadership wins out: **Leadership is simply influence**. Period. I love how refreshingly simple that is. It's not put on a pedestal or churched up with flowery prose.

Leadership = Influence.

Merriam-Webster defines influence as "the power or capacity of causing an effect." Over the last decade of experiencing, researching, and debating leadership in military, academic, and private industry settings, there are two transformative insights I've experienced on the theme of Leadership.

The first insight is that IF leadership is influence, THEN each person is a leader because we constantly affect anyone or anything else with which we interact. We interact with people and things every second of our life. Every action taken or not taken. Every word said or not said. Every decision or non-decision carries with it the power and capacity to cause an effect. When a decision or action is viewed through this lens, the lens of a leader, the weight it carries increases. Intentionality increases. The second- and third-order effects of the words you speak and the actions you take come into sharper focus.

With this first insight, I began to view each person around me as a leader. I began to see just how powerful the individual contributor is who brings energy, positivity, and joy to their work. Conversely, I began to see how powerful and influential the cynical, status-quo-loving colleague is. But leadership is not limited to the professional arena. I am inspired by the child who says good morning to everyone on the way to school. Or the begging, homeless veteran on the corner. Going through your day, I bet you can find thousands of examples of people influencing others and being influenced by an interaction. The power and capacity for any one of us to cause an effect is astronomical. We are influencing and being influenced by every single interaction.

I was in 2nd grade the first time I understood what the word "leader" means. I was in trouble and my teacher, Mrs. Bailey, was scolding me because I was distracting the class. Mrs. Bailey had pulled me out of the classroom and was lecturing me in the hallway. She was using words like "rabble-rouser" and "distraction." But she also did one of the most impactful things of my life: she explained that I have influence. In effect, she had helped me see the invisible blue yarn that connected me to those around me.

The other kids were being affected by my choices. I was doing things like pretending to snore to get a laugh. Or purposefully dropping my pencil on the ground to cause a distraction. Or trying to get my best friend Travis's attention during math work. Mrs. Bailey explained that she needed my help. I could continue to be a distraction and disrupt the classroom, or I could help other kids learn by staying calm and attentive. I had influence, but also the responsibility for that influence. I was causing an effect. This moment of self-awareness completely changed the way I viewed the world.

This view of everyone having influence continues to shape my worldview. The defining experiences of my life validate this insight: growing up in a military family; being active in multiple sports as a child; attending and graduating from the Air Force Academy; serving as an Active Duty Air Force Intelligence Officer in Special Operations and the National Security Agency; and now in the role I have in a top-tier Silicon Valley organization. And as my most important role as a husband and father, I am influenced by and recognize my influence on my wife and children.

The second transformative insight on Leadership is that IF leadership is influence, **THEN we are also continuously leading ourselves**. Every time we take action to set our own conditions for success, we are leading ourselves. Do you set an alarm? Have a few ways to remind you to accomplish a task? Set out workout clothes the night before? Create a shopping list? Set aside time for meditation or self-reflection? All of these are very small decisions we take to put ourselves in better positions to achieve our goals. If you are looking for hundreds of pages on habits, rituals, and methods for influencing oneself on a daily basis then I would recommend Tim Ferris's book, Tools of Titans.

Have you ever heard the maxim fake it until you make it? There is evidence supporting this point of view. There are decades of research underpinning something called Behavior Activation theory which concludes that one of the most impactful ways someone can overcome an episode of depression is through acting as if they are not depressed (Dimidjian, Barrera Jr., Martell, Munoz, and Lewinsohn, 2011). It turns out the concept of influencing your own mind is a very real and impactful mindset to adopt. We are neurologically wired for being influenced by and influencing others. Before exploring how and why our consciousness is organized for influence in Part II of this book, there are a few more conclusions to draw from Mr. Barrett's Brooklyn Heights classroom and the episode with the blue yarn.

There is something uniquely and fundamentally human about the story of the blue yarn being passed around in class. It's not that we influence one another. Although, that is fundamental to leadership. The something that is unique about this story is written between the lines. A nuance that is unsaid.

The something is that we can, if we choose to, take responsibility for our influence. Our species is unique in that we are able to think about our own thinking. The technical term for this is metacognition, and it enables us to reflect on the past, imagine ourselves in the future, and use both analytical and intuitive reasoning to adjust our thinking. Ironically, scientists know more about the cosmos than they do our own minds, but one thing **neuroscientists do know is that we can rewire our own mindsets, our habits, and our behaviors.**

Breaking a single habit or changing a single cognitive bias is a hard thing to do. Harder still is zooming out and realizing **you are an ever-changing process, a verb, not a noun**. Whether we like it or not, we are constantly interacting with the world around us and our mind's interpretation of the world around us. This doesn't depend on things like having a "growth mindset." Unless you have zero interactions with your own world and have zero thoughts in your brain, then you are ever-changing from one minute to the next minute, day, month, year, decade, and throughout your life.

The point is that internally and externally, we are bombarded by distractions and noise every single day. We can get lost in reactive-mode where we simply respond to stimuli. Have you ever had a list of three things on your to-do list for the day and then all hell breaks loose, leaving you reviewing your list at the end of the day wondering where the day went? It is hard to influence ourselves and institute some cognitive control over our own minds and lives. Even altering a single habit is a complex, systemic problem that is not straightforward at all. We need help.

We have to elevate ourselves above the discrete choices of our day-to-day to realize that those choices, behaviors, and thoughts are forming a system of action or influence whether we take responsibility for them or not. In other words, even if it is happening without your awareness, **your life is a system of evolving influence.** Every moment we are alive we pull on the yarn and are pulled by the yarn. Once we become aware of this it shifts our paradigm. We can see our consciousness as an opportunity. Every moment we can choose to be pulled and pull the yarn in directions that we choose. With self-responsibility and self-compassion, **we can create and sustain a virtuous cycle within our own lives.**

In this book, I'll introduce a system of influence that can be a guide for leading oneself. I am also hopeful this system is a philosophy of leadership that scales up so we can take responsibility and positively influence our children, partners, friends, teams, and organizations. My argument is based on two assumptions:

1.   Leadership equals influence

2.   Taking responsibility for your own influence must be a deliberate, conscious, and continuous choice

Therefore, my hypothesis is that every single person is a leader who can optimize their own systems of influence through Awareness, Inspiration, and Accountability. We are all wired to lead. But the first step in leadership is taking responsibility.

Chapter 2: RESPONSIBILITY

"Ultimately, man should not ask what the meaning of his life is, but rather must recognize that it is he who is asked. In a word, each man is questioned by life; and he can only answer to life by answering for his own life; to life he can only respond by being responsible."

- Viktor Frankl, Man's Search for Meaning

What change are you seeking in the world?

Where are you at now?

Where do you want to be?

How are you going to get there?

The opposite of leadership isn't followership. The opposite of leadership is helplessness. Leaders take responsibility.

Responsibility for...

How they think. How they act. Where they are at now. Where they want to be. And how they are going to get there.

The current state. The process. The outcome.

The framework scales up as well. A leader of a team takes responsibility.

Responsibility for....

Where the team is now. Where the team wants to be. And how they are going to get there.

The current state. The outcome. The process.

Do you know the difference between a good leader and a bad leader?

Good leadership starts with taking responsibility.

Someone who doesn't lead chooses apathy, or to "just go with the flow," or to not consider where they are at, or ignores the process, et cetera. There are a million reasons why someone chooses to not take responsibility.

But an absolutely CRITICAL realization is that both are CHOICES.

You either CHOOSE responsibility.

Or you CHOOSE something else.

You aren't off the hook if you shrink into the background. You aren't off the hook if you are "just a team member." You aren't off the hook if you are "a relatively junior member of the organization."

"Oh, I'm just a teammate."

"Oh, but I'm just an Airman."

"Oh, I'm just a Private First Class."

Oh, but I'm just an individual contributor."

I'd like to request we remove "just" from the English language. Saying "just" is choosing to avoid responsibility.

Step 1: Choose to take responsibility.

Step 2: Don't stop.

And don't half-ass your decision. Do you know why? **Because you are the one you've been waiting for.** You are the leader you need right now. The leader that empathizes with you; the leader that imagines and paints a vision of a better version of your world; the leader that regulates and manages your time to help you accomplish your greatest goals and higher purpose. The leader that applies meaning to how you experience the world. It is worth saying multiple times: you are the one you've been waiting for. Decide to take responsibility.

But really decide. Don't decide like you decide to get a gym membership. Decide like you mean it. The word decision is from the Latin "to cut off" and literally means to cut off all other choices. And that's what we are talking about. Choosing responsibility is a "should I amputate my arm" kind of decision and not a "should I change my shirt" kind of decision.

Chapter 3:

DEMOCRATIZING LEADERSHIP

"So, influenced by these advisors and this hope, I have at length allowed my friends to publish the work, as they had long besought me to do."

- Nikolai Copernicus

In 1543, Nikolai Copernicus was on his deathbed when he was handed the first published copy of the book he had written. It was a book based on his own questioning, observations, and hypotheses. The Polish polymath, Copernicus, articulated his point of view three decades before this moment. But the truths articulated in the book remained unpublished until he was on his deathbed because, at the time, he wasn't the one responsible for scientific truth.

Up until that time, the truth was dictated from on high by the monarchs, lords, and bishops. So-called leaders who dictated truth to the uneducated masses. Copernicus was justifiably afraid of ridicule, shame, and persecution. There was no precedent set for a layman uncovering and publishing facts regarding the world. His book blasphemously articulated his conclusion that the Sun, and not the Earth, was at the center of the known universe.

The famous book, On the Revolutions of the Heavenly Spheres, was the first domino to fall in the centuries-long Scientific Revolution that finally democratized truth across disciplines such as physics, biology, psychology, and neuroscience. The Scientific Revolution is still ongoing. I say ongoing because there are many parts of the world where new observations, evidence, or ideas are dismissed outright due to the position or rank of the speaker. **But here's what we know: truth is truth. Every individual has the opportunity to discover for him or herself what is and what is not.**

No one should have to publish their life's work on their deathbed. Or worse, take their ideas to the grave. I believe each and every human being has their own version of On the Revolutions of Heavenly Spheres inside them. As Viktor

Frankl stated, we answer the question of the meaning of life by being responsible for our life. It is a choice to manifest our greatest dreams and highest hopes through our thoughts, feelings, and ultimately decisions and behaviors.

We need a Leadership Revolution.

This involves each person viewing themselves as the Chief Executive Officer of their lives across all domains: personal, professional, emotional, spiritual, physical, financial, etc.. Back to the definition of leadership:

Leadership = **influence.**

Leadership is **choosing to be responsible** for the influence we have on ourselves and our world.

How did we get to the point where leadership is associated only with an elite few or those "in charge?" Harvard Business Review (HBR) published an article titled <u>Why Anyone Should be Led by You</u>, and it is recognized as one of HBR's top ten articles on leadership of all time. In the article, the authors review the history of leadership theory to consolidate and articulate the four most important leadership qualities. The authors "ransacked" the three main leadership theories:

1. Trait theory- extensive evidence disproved this hypothesis that effective leaders were tall or short, male or female, or some other genetic trait (this theory includes the 1800s Great Man Theory)

2. Style theory- extensive studies disproved this hypothesis that one specific style was more effective at accomplishing a goal than another

3. Contingency theory- extensive studies proved that each situation required a unique leadership approach

The authors come to what they call an "unexpected" conclusion of four main qualities that make an effective leader:

1. An effective leader is approachable and reveals their humanity through humility and demonstrating vulnerability

2. An effective leader relies on their intuition (Khaneman's System 1, which we will discuss later) to help determine when and how to act

3. An effective leader practices tough empathy- caring deeply about their workers and the work they do

4. An effective leader recognizes they have unique strengths and capitalizes on what is uniquely them

Okay. I was on an airplane when I read this article and started to laugh in anger. That's right. I laughed in anger at the authors' "unexpected conclusions." One of my favorite T.S. Eliot quotes is

We shall not cease from exploration, and the end of all our exploring will be to arrive where we started and know the place for the first time.

At the end of exhaustive research and decades of leadership consulting experience, the authors come to the conclusion that (paraphrasing in my own words) **to be an effective leader you have to be a good human who wants to share the best of yourself with the people around you in order to achieve something greater than yourself.** T.S. Eliot was right. After 150 years of management and leadership theory study, we come to arrive looking inwardly, at our own humanity to find the good in us that can inspire ourselves and those around us.

The leadership revolution is one by one, each of us taking responsibility for and then shaping the impact we want our influence to have on our world.

Everyone is a leader. And adopting that mindset is absolutely, transformational to individuals, communities, teams, and organizations.

An exploration of leading ourselves and others has to begin with our systems of consciousness. If we are leading ourselves, we are creating a change in our own character, thoughts and feelings in order to drive certain choices and behaviors. When we lead another person, we are influencing their character, thoughts, and feelings in order to drive certain choices and behaviors. Our consciousness makes up most, if not all, of our "self." It turns out we have an evolutionary system of influence composed of certain neural networks that can be leveraged to direct us in the direction of our values and desired end states. Our minds have the composition to allow us to understand where we are at, imagine where we want to go, take responsibility for the path from here to there, and deal with unforeseen variables we encounter along the way. To take responsibility for our influence, it is helpful to understand where that System of Influence begins and ends, as well as understand how to leverage and maximize our leadership potential.

PART II

WIRED TO LEAD

Chapter 4:

SYSTEM OF INFLUENCE

"If a factory is torn down but the rationality which produced it is left standing, then that rationality will simply produce another factory. If a revolution destroys a government, but the systematic patterns of thought that produced the government are left intact, then those patterns will repeat themselves.... There's so much talk about the system. And so little understanding."
- Robert Pirsig, Zen and the Art of Motorcycle Maintenance

Systems thinking as a discipline emphasizes that problems and solutions never exist in a vacuum, but have context and interrelationships. Furthermore, there is a known hierarchy of thinking that begins with looking at an individual **event** in isolation. The next level is being able to view **patterns** of events or trends over time. This helps determine causality and correlation, but also impacts our ability to forecast and make decisions based on probabilities. Finally, and I think of this last level as being able to "see the matrix:" a **systems view**, where you can see an event or pattern from the perspective of the elements, interrelationships, and function/purpose of the system. As Peter Senge in The Fifth Discipline discusses in depth, this is the lens that allows us to truly identify the root causes of problems and fundamental solutions instead of symptomatic problems and short-term solutions that mask the symptoms. **So, instead of viewing leadership or influence as an event, or a pattern, it is critical to view leadership as a system**. A system that resides in our consciousness, is made up of interrelated elements, and has a set purpose.

Interestingly, consciousness is both the source and the destination of influence (leadership). Every element of our character, our self, is rooted in our consciousness. Likewise, if we are inspired to take action, or change our minds, or follow guidance, or feel motivated, or have a lightbulb moment, then that shift is happening in our minds.

When it comes to leadership, our minds have three neural networks that form the operating system of leadership. This operating system exists at two levels in the human mind: the intuitive, unconscious level (System 1), and the rational, conscious level (System 2) (TIME; Kahneman). Understanding the operating system and two levels at which the system operates is fundamental to taking responsibility for your influence.

In the last couple decades, neuroscientists mapped this system of influence in our consciousness. In a 2019 Time Magazine Special Edition on The Science of Creativity, the author details how scientists discovered the three neural networks that work together to form one's ability to create. The first network (what I refer to as Awareness)is…

"…the salience network, which works by toggling between the anterior insula and the dorsal anterior cingulate cortex. The insula is what helps you monitor the world around you using multiple information streamed, and the cingulate helps you sieve some of that out, concentrating only on what you need." (p. 16)

In other words, the salience network's function is to monitor your world, internal and external, as well as regulating what is monitored. The second network (what I refer to as Inspiration) is…

"…the imagination network, which allows the brain to do previously untried things with the information the executive-attention network has provided. Here, not only are the parietal and the prefrontal involved but also the medial temporal, which is involved in memory, and the posterior cingulate, which has a role in planning and daydreaming." (p. 15)

The imagination network heavily functions off of memory as a foundation, but is also activated when planning and day-dreaming occurs. And finally, the third network (what I refer to as Accountability)

"…the executive-attention network is where the muscle work of creativity gets done. It's that network that helps us do the fiercely focused studying, reading and practicing that gives us a mastery of, say, language or music or color and light....Executive-attention requires close communication between the prefrontal cortex, which gathers and absorbs incoming information, and the posterior parietal cortex, which integrates different data streams from different sensory systems." (p. 15)

The executive-attention network is where shit gets done. The ability to focus. The ability to stay focused and reach milestones and targets.

This system of influence, awareness - inspiration - accountability forms the foundation of one's ability to take responsibility for their influence. Imagine trying to get from your apartment or house to a doctor appointment across town. What do you need to get from here to there? Well, you need to know where your house is (awareness- where you are at now) relative to the doctor's office (inspiration- where you want to go), and you need to have some measures along the way that allow you to know whether you are on track (accountability). Missing one of those three elements will slow you down tremendously if not completely cause failure in accomplishing what you are trying to do.

Once aware of these neural networks that combine to form our ability to affect a change, I began to view my own influence and those around me through this leadership system. I'm an optimist and a dreamer. It is very easy to stay in inspiration mode for me. I imagine if I could have an fMRI machine attached to my head constantly measuring my neural network activity over the course of a month, then well over 60% of the time would be my imagination network being active. For whatever reason, I think I am naturally inclined to that element of my system of influence. I can look back at my development over the last two decades and see how I had to be very intentional about developing self-awareness, empathy, and self-management techniques that allowed me to effectively turn vision into reality. But that is a very specific example about me. Everyone is going to be naturally inclined one way or another.

We all know friends, families, colleagues, and managers who are all talk and very little action. High in inspiration but low on accountability. Or the person who wants to spend very little time imagining or brainstorming and just wants to descend into the particulars of getting things done and hitting milestones. High in accountability and low in inspiration. Or the person that seems to have zero self-awareness or ability to empathize. Low in awareness. These are tendencies that each and everyone has. And to be honest, unless a person invests in their ability to be self-aware and others-aware, then there is little chance that they will develop the other two elements.

Luckily, through human evolution, we do not always have to be completely conscious and intentional of the neural networks at work. Our minds are hardwired to put as much as possible into auto-pilot. We develop our habits, biases, and preferences based on our brain's constant fight for efficiency. All habits are cognitive biases that have been moved from the fully conscious part of our minds (System 2) to what is termed the adaptive unconscious part of our brains (System 1).

We all know people who seem to have it all together. People who make it look so easy. And there is an increasing interest in studying the tactics and techniques of those "superhumans" among us. Author and entrepreneur Tim Ferris comes to mind as someone who has made it his life's work to deconstruct mastery and excellence. What Ferris and others have found is when you zoom in to that seemingly **deep well of self-discipline, self-awareness, and motivation, you find there is actually a chain of habits, rituals, and biases which act as a system of influence that continuously moves the individuals in pursuit of their goals.** The biases and behaviors are second nature and can be found in the center of their brain in a piece of brain tissue called the basal ganglia (Duhigg).

In Charles Duhigg's <u>Power of Habit</u>, he discusses the basal ganglia, a part of our brain located near the "center of the onion" as the primary regulator of behaviors and actions. Interestingly, this same basal ganglia is a critical part of what Gladwell, Wilson, and Kahneman refer to as the adaptive unconscious (i.e. System 1, or the Fast Brain). System 1 is the automatic, reflexive, and intuitive portion of our brain. The conscious part, or System 2, is the slow, deliberate, reflective, and thoughtful part of our brain.

An easy way to remember System 1 versus System 2 is to think about it in the context of human evolution. System 1 came first, and System 2 developed second and continues to develop today. From an evolutionary standpoint, System 1 developed 10 million years ago and was in charge of flight or fight responses to ensure our ancestors' survival. System 2 developed over the last 2 million years of human evolution due to higher protein diets, the formations of civilizations, and the increasingly complex nature of our world.

We slowly (over 8 million years) began to think more long-term, deliberately, and proactively. Our species didn't necessarily need to only react, fight, or flight. System 2 was able to be more reflective and aware of experiences, imagine alternatives, and develop long-term milestones that could lead to long-term success. But there is still a tremendous utility to System 1.

For the sake of efficiency, our brain is trying to move our processes, thoughts, and ultimately behaviors toward auto-pilot (System 1). Although only 2% of our body mass, the brain uses up 25% of our ~90 Watts of energy we require every day to sustain life. So this process of moving as much as possible to System 1 in the form of a routine, bias, and a habit allows the brain to use less energy and frees up the upper, conscious brain (System 2) to be deliberate and thoughtful. Think about some of the basic activities we have in System 1: breathing, walking, speaking, reading, etc. These automated thoughts and behaviors are simply heuristics: mental shortcuts that help us operate as efficiently as possible in order to make room for the variations, iterations, and selections that occur in System 2.

This ability for System 2 to influence System 1 is a manifestation of the plasticity of our brains. Plasticity can be thought of as our ability to "change our minds." This can be in the form of our behaviors, habits, underlying assumptions, paradigms, and ultimately our own character. This plastic nature of our brain ensures that we can continue evolving, changing our minds, and potentially advancing as a species. System 1 houses our habits, biases, and routines. System 2 houses our ability to think about choosing something different. We are quite literally wired to lead ourselves.

But what about that stubborn person who never changes their minds, loves the status quo, and rejects every opportunity to introduce an evolution or change? That person has the same wiring as those superhumans who seem to have extraordinary control of their consciousness. While System 1 is not entirely in our conscious-control, System 2 is wholly dependent on our own free will. **One has to make a conscious choice to consider differing viewpoints, a change in a habit, an attitude toward a specific externality, etc.**

The system of influence operating at both the conscious and unconscious levels of our mind is how we devolve, maintain unchanged, or evolve. There is a metaphor I have found helpful in visualizing the context in which we exist. Imagine yourself as a tree. Let's say you are a 23-year-old reading this. Then you are a 23-year-old tree that has grown roots, a tree trunk, branches, and leaves. Your behaviors and actions are the most visible aspect of you. The leaves are the most noticeable aspects of YOU. However, the leaves are shaped by and rely on the branches, which represent your mental heuristics, biases, and habits. Your behaviors and actions are a manifestation of those mental shortcuts.

The branches are shaped and rely on the tree trunk, which represents your character, which is the summation of your self: holding up your principles, assumptions, thoughts, feelings, behaviors, and actions. Your habits, choices, and actions are manifestations of your character. Finally, the root system of your tree is underpinned by the values you hold highest. They are unseen but foundational to your character, habits, and actions. The mind's system of influence allows us to shape and reshape this tree. It is through becoming conscious and deliberate about our values, biases, habits, and choices that we can develop new biases and habits that better serve our values. Simply stated, we leverage our three neural networks to influence our life. First, we become aware of a decision, behavior, or habit we currently have. Second, we imagine a vision for the ideal decision, behavior, or habit. And finally, we implement measurements, milestones, and management in order to get us from here to there.

Chapter 5: AWARENESS

Where am I now?

"Get clear about exactly what it is that you need to learn and exactly what you need to do to learn it. BEING CLEAR KILLS FEAR. Make it thy business to know thyself, which is the most difficult lesson in the world."

- Miguel Cervantes, Spanish author, dramatist, and poet

The first pillar of the system of influence is Awareness. The world around us is constantly changing. We are not only bombarded by external stimuli from the world but also our thoughts, feelings, desires that are internal as well. With these circumstances in mind, it logically follows that we need a way to check in from time to time with our self. Take stock of our current state. To take our own temperature. To measure where we are at. While mindfulness and meditation seem to be the latest fad, there are a couple of foundational studies which point to the life-long importance of awareness.

One of the most famous studies is based on an experiment called the Marshmallow Test, led by Stanford University professor Walter Mischel. The Marshmallow Test is an experiment accomplished by having a researcher in a room with a child, and the child sits down and there is a single marshmallow on the table in front of them. The researcher lets the child know that they are going to have to leave the room for fifteen minutes, and the child has a choice: they can either go ahead and eat the single marshmallow now, or when the researcher returns they will bring a second marshmallow and the child can then eat two marshmallows. So the choice is one marshmallow now or two marshmallows in fifteen minutes.

The long-term results of the study are incredibly insightful. The children who were willing to wait fifteen minutes and have two marshmallows were measurably more successful in life 20-30 years later as measured by "life outcomes," including SAT scores, educational attainment, body mass index

(BMI). What quality or characteristic were these kids actually demonstrating when they chose to wait fifteen minutes? There is one more research study that is complementary and necessary to fully round out this concept of Awareness.

Dr. Robert Kagan is the Professor of Adult Learning and Psychology at Harvard. Decades of research has led him and his colleagues to develop the Subject Object Theory. This theory states that the single most important factor in adult growth and development is the ability to be able to remove ourselves from being the thing observed (object) and become the observer (subject) of our thoughts, desires, and feelings. The term that has become more popularized for this kind of theory is metacognition, or thinking about our thinking.

The Subject-Object Theory and the Marshmallow Test are two of the fundamental studies highlighting the importance of metacognition to our growth and success as individuals. Interestingly, neuroscientists have also narrowed down our ability to be "aware" in the broadest sense to not only the salience neural network previously mentioned, but specifically to a portion of our brain called the insula. And, in studies over time, neuroscientists have measured that a person focuses on developing skills we refer to as Emotional Intelligence (or EQ, which includes self- and social-awareness), the neural activity in the insula increases, like a muscle building over time. Similar to how athletes develop their leg muscles by using squat exercises to generate power during their competition, scientists have shown that a person can develop their insula using mindfulness techniques such as focusing all their attention on the beat of their heart or their breath in order to increase their EQ.

Two significant lessons emerge from the Marshmallow Test and Subject-Object Theory:

1. Being able to think about our own thinking and thereby transcending our thoughts, feelings, and desires allow us to rise above both the external and internal noise and take stock of who we are, where we are at in our life, and how it compares to the last time we

practiced this awareness.

2.   Being aware and practicing awareness as a skillset or a habit can be developed over time like a muscle (or atrophy like a muscle). This makes the kind of mindfulness and awareness accessible to every single one of our species.

In its simplest form, step 1 of the system of influence is to ask yourself "who am I now? Where am I now?" By doing this, you are setting the foundation to ask the follow-up question: "who do I want to be? How does the current state compare to the desired end state?" This alludes to the second element, Inspiration, but that is how the system works. All elements are interrelated and none of them are exclusive.

In effect, you are turning the lights on in your own mind. This takes advantage of something psychologists term the Hawthorne Effect, which is a phenomenon noticed during studies of factory workers in the 1920s. Researchers experimented with the productivity of workers by increasing the brightness of the lighting and measuring the change in productivity. Productivity increased. But curiously, productivity also increased when the lighting was decreased. What the researchers finally realized was regardless of what changes took place in the experiments, it was the workers' knowledge they were being observed that was increasing the productivity. This phenomenon resembles the Subject-Object Theory and is also critical to the third element of the system of influence: Accountability.

But notice the implication of the Hawthorne effect: productivity increases only when there is the perception of being "under observation." The least effective strategy for having self-awareness would be to make it a discrete event. This is akin to wanting to become a runner but trying to go out for one really long run. As discussed in the previous chapter, the key is to build awareness as a habit.

Chapter 6: INSPIRATION

Where do I want to be?

"Those ideas that please me I retain in memory, and am accustomed, as I have been told, to hum them to myself. If I continue in this way, it soon occurs to me how I may turn this or that morsel to account so as to make a good dish of it... All this fires my soul."

- Wolfgang Amadeus Mozart

Inspiration is the fire of our soul. I love that. I recently asked a friend of mine when the last time she felt inspired was. Her response was "six years ago." I asked again if there were really no times within the last six years when she felt inspired and she responded "no." This solidified for me how different each one of us begins our leadership journey. Inspiration is easy for me. I am inspired by the sunrise, by the smile and kindness of a stranger, by a daily Zen Calendar, and I can go on and on. But that's me. I have made inspiration into a habit and ascribe inspirational meaning to everyday experiences. My development needed, and still needs, to focus on accountability and awareness. But my friend is working on activating her imagination network. She is doing this by reflecting on where she wants to be. Where does she picture herself in two years? What about that moment six years ago inspired her and how does she find that more often? Aristotle said "Excellence is a habit, not an act." This rings true for leadership, awareness, inspiration, and accountability. **The goal should be to make a habit out of them, not discrete events or acts.**

Fascinatingly, neuroscientists have discovered a number of traits of our brains in recent decades:

1. The vast majority of our brain activity is occurring intrinsically. In other words, the source of the majority of our brain activity is not in response to any outside stimulus, but rather an inner dialogue, our

imagination, and our daydreams.

2.   There is a natural selection process going on inside our minds
      where we create spontaneous variations that the conscious portion of
      our brains can then effectively 'choose' from. Over time, these
      variations become part of System 1, or instinctual.

This research blew my mind, actually. **There is a biological and
neurological purpose for our imagination.** Our daydreams. Our weirdest,
strangest, and far-flung thoughts and feelings have a purpose. In order to
discover new and better ideas, you have to have a lot of weird and bad ideas.
And that process of high variance, selection, iteration, variance, selection and
so on has been going on in the 3 pounds of matter between our ears for the last
10 million years.

This is also why diversity of experience and thought is so important.
Biologists know high variance builds out resilient ecosystems and species that
are able to accidentally innovate so better ways of life are consistently selected
for. This is why inspiration is so critical to this process. It is the engine for our
growth. Our rational, thoughtful, and deliberate System 2 was designed to
consider alternatives, explore unknowns, and dream of the possible so our
consciousness can also accidentally innovate and find better ways of life.

A lot of the structure I put around inspiration takes the form of asking
myself "what does winning look like?" I had a military instructor who used to
ask a similar question: "what does Christmas morning look like?" It's a
shorthand for providing the vision in your imagination to hold on so you can
do the gap analysis between where you are now and where you want to be. For
my marriage, for instance, I always tell my wife that the vision is, at 80 years
old, we are sitting in rocking chairs, sipping iced tea and watching our great-
grandchildren playing on the lawn. This encapsulates our priorities and helps
provide the vision for my marriage and family life. What about the vision for
work, or for health, or mind, or body, or spirit? These various domains each
need inspiration to motivate and provide a direction for your energy.

There is not going to be a one-size-fits-all method for finding or staying inspired. Each person finds inspiration in their own way. But it is important to seek it out. Do not sit back and allow days, weeks, or years to go by without feeling inspired. Some people need to make a long, linear list of what "Christmas morning" looks like. Others need a blank whiteboard and a pot of coffee. Still others' need to seek extensive council with friends and family or spend some time in solitude on a long forest trail. We each apply our own method for inspiration.

Similar to developing our insula to increase awareness, we can deliberately increase activity in our inspiration (imagination) network through developing habits of inspiration based on your unique understanding of what inspires you. The more you actively seek out inspiration, the more inspired you will be. That is an obvious statement, but still profound. We need to continually revisit the imagination network to fuel our system of influence. Awareness provides you the sense for where you are at now and Inspiration provides you a sense for where you want to go. But the three elements of the system of influence require balance. You aren't leading anything if you don't provide some aspects of accountability to help you get from your current state to your desired end state.

Chapter 7: ACCOUNTABILITY

How am I going to get there?

"Things which matter most should never be at the mercy of things that matter least."

- Johann Wolfgang von Goethe, German writer and statesman

My wife, Maggie, hates the term hustle. When she thinks of hustle she thinks of the "rat race" of a life where you never take a breath but are always on-on-on. I love the term hustle. Because all of a sudden, discipline is cool. Focus is cool. Maggie and I recently had a conversation where I challenged her negative connotation of discipline and hustle. She owns her own yoga business and I asked her "Doesn't yoga involve certain structure and key, deliberate steps to help you achieve a certain outcome of your practice?" I felt I had won the argument as I usually feel, but of course in reality I've never won an argument with my wife. Accountability and wrapping your mind around the concepts of self-management, structure, and building out milestones for the change you seek to effect is the third element of the system of influence.

Accountability to me is measuring what matters so you are more likely to achieve the thing you desire or the effect you are trying to achieve. Measurements and milestones are a life-hack to help keep you on track and ensure you eat the proverbial elephant one bit at a time. The executive-attention (accountability) network is where shit gets done. There are hundreds of books and articles written each year on specific tools that can be used for self-management. But there are a number of studies highlighting the important role of accountability to achieving influence.

First, is the Hawthorne effect discussed in the Awareness chapter. By turning the lights on in your own mind, you increase your chances of accomplishing that which you set out to achieve. Any sense of observation, such as writing your goals and milestones down or sharing them with a peer or via social media are various methods for increasing accountability.

Second, there is a Harvard Business School study showing that the 3% of MBA students who consistently wrote down their goals ended up making ten times as much money as the other 97% of students combined. When first gathering information from the students in the study, the researchers found the following breakouts:

- 84% had no specific goals at all

- 13% had goals but they were not committed to paper

- 3% had clear, written goals and plans to accomplish them

The studies we now have from neuroscientists on how our neural networks shape our levels of influence suggest these 3% of students did not have isolated acts of accountability. Instead, we can infer that the 3% had developed habits of accountability that were active enough to operate at the unconscious part of their minds.

Accountability activity in our minds helps us stay focused on what we are trying to achieve. This neural network activity also supports the other two elements. In each of the other elements, awareness and inspiration, there has been an emphasis on establishing awareness and inspiration practices in order to move the activity from the conscious to unconscious level. Accountability activities are the method with which we create and sustain the awareness and inspiration practices.

The system of influence is the balance between three questions being consistently asked:

- Where am I now?

- Where do I want to be?

- How am I going to get there?

These questions, their answers, and more importantly the process set in motion is the foundation for democratizing leadership. This process is what allows us to take responsibility for our influence and begin deliberately leading ourselves, and others, through our daily choices and behaviors.

Chapter 10:

CONCLUSION

"No great improvements in the lot of mankind are possible until a great change takes place in the fundamental constitution of their modes of thought."
- John Stuart Mill, Philosopher

There is not a cookbook recipe for becoming a leader. What gets me to a point of being totally involved, inspired, and growing in life as a leader is not the same thing that will get my neighbor, or co-worker, or brother, or you for that matter. Decades and sometimes centuries of research on consciousness, management, leadership, and happiness demonstrate there is NOT ONE BEST WAY. That's the catch-22 of free will. We are all leaders because we inherently have influence. But we are taking our potential impact, our vision for a better future, our ideas, our laughter, our lessons, and our best selves to the grave with us if we don't take responsibility for that influence.

Step 1 is taking responsibility. Step 2 is not stopping.

The fact that we are influencing ourselves, being influenced by others, and influencing others is obvious. But it is so ubiquitous that it is taken for granted by the majority of the population. It reminds me of a speech by David Foster Wallace.

At the 2005 commencement speech at Kenyon College, author David Foster Wallace told the story of an older fish passing two younger fish in the ocean. As he passes by, the older fish looks at the younger fish and says "morning boys, how's the water?" The younger fish swim on for a little while before one of them turns to the other and says "what the hell is water?"

This concept of leadership as influence over ourselves and everyone else in our lives is as real and hidden in plain sight as the water for the fish. As Wallace explains, we have to keep reminding ourselves:

"This is water."

"This is water."

So...what change are you seeking in the world? How might you regularly increase awareness as it relates to that change? How might you regularly imagine and inspire yourself with that vision? And how might you leverage self-accountability tools in order to maximize your chances of achieving that vision? This is the wiring that already exists in our minds. It is a natural-born capacity to lead that we must simply point toward our highest values and visions.

There is nothing stopping you right now. Go make that change happen. Then go inspire others to lead. Go create leaders with every interaction you have, unlocking the potential for others to realize the change they seek in the world. A leadership revolution consists of democratizing leadership just as the Scientific Revolution democratized truth. Leadership is accessible to all. We now understand there are three key neural networks that go into leadership: awareness, inspiration, and accountability. And these three neural networks operate at two levels within our minds: conscious and unconscious. Leveraging those facts, an individual is able to not only view their world from the lens of a leader, but also begin to optimize the system of influence that exists within the neural networks and at both the conscious and unconscious levels.

Sadly, recent studies show that only 8% of people achieve their goals, over 65% of employees are disengaged at work, and the average American is just above average on a scale of not happy to happy. But what if every individual viewed themselves as a leader? What if every individual acted as if they are a leader, took responsibility, and leveraged their intrinsic ability to affect the change they seek?

My hope is that we are at the beginning of an upward trajectory of this Leadership Revolution. I'm optimistic because of my experiences in special operations and the Silicon Valley organizations. Scientists have only begun to discover the nature of our consciousness and the neural networks which form it. I'm hopeful this research can continue to knock our self-doubt, fear, and unwillingness to change.

I truly believe everyone is a leader. You are the one you have been waiting for. You have the tools at your disposal. Now is the fun part of deciding what change do you seek in the world. And...Go!

THAT IS THE END OF THE BOOK